Conservation Cody

Nadine Vander Wall

DEDICATED TO LUCKY,
THE BICHON FRISE.

Cody's life would be dull without fresh air, clean water, trees, and tall grass.

Everything was going great, as it usually did. But then, on one cloudy, dark day, Cody learned about a very scary word. The word… pollution! Pollution made Cody upset because he wants to help, not hurt the environment.

After a long afternoon of thinking and watching squirrels, Cody still wondered how a little puppy like him, could stop pollution and keep the environment safe.

After daydreaming, Cody finally fell asleep under a tree. He had an important dream that told him how to help our environment. Naturally, as a nature lover, Cody was happy to finally figure out how he could help save our beautiful planet.

Now Cody wants to show you what he can do!

During the winter, Cody wears a sweater inside the house. This reduces the energy and electricity used to heat the inside of a house. He always remembers to turn off the lights when he leaves the room because that helps save energy too.

Cody puts his old food in the compost at home. In the spring he has rich soil for the garden.

When he goes on a picnic, he puts his food into containers that can be washed and used again. Now there is less plastic in the landfill. Some garbage, like plastic, never decomposes.

When Cody gets dirty, he uses just enough water to get clean.

Cody puts used paper, pop cans, glass jars, and plastic into the recycle bin. He is doing his part!

He even trades and shares toys with his friends. He always gets new toys and doesn't even have to go to the store. He has so much fun!

Most of all, Cody likes to walk to all of his favorite places, or ride his bike. If he has to drive, he tries to carpool with friends who are going the same way.

Cody does his part because he loves nature! You can do your part to help the planet as well. Follow Cody's habits and you can keep playing in the fresh air and swimming in the clean water too!

If people waste, and throw garbage on the ground or in the water, they are polluting. Polluting makes Cody sad because pollution ruins the earth. Cody knows you can do your part just like him, so that we can live in a beautiful, clean world!

THE END

conservation: the protection of animals, plants, and natural resources

decompose: to cause something to be slowly destroyed and broken down by natural processes

habit: something that a person does often in a regular and repeated way

pollution: the action or process of making land, water, air, etc., dirty and not safe or suitable to use

recycle: to make something new from (something that has been used before)

definitions from: http://www.learnersdictionary.com

To conserve energy and protect the planet, I...

_____

_____

_____

_____